The Happy Mason Jar

by Alyssa Cremeans

"God can do anything, you know — far more than you could ever imagine or guess or request in your wildest dreams! He does it not by pushing us around but by working within us, his Spirit deeply and gently within us." Ephesians 3:20 (MSG)

Thank You

To the team who made this book come to life.

Publishing by Happy Mason Jar, LLC

Photography by Katherine Mindel

Cover Design by Devin Cremeans

Dessert Styling by Melodie Paulsen

Social Media Marketing by Trendy Lemon

Floral Design by On Thai, Surroundings Floral

Kitchen Designs by Carrie Hoffman and Jessica Dailey

Wine Expertise by George Ryals, All Star Wine & Spirits

Copyedit by Jenna Nelson Patton, Reedsy Publishing

Proofread by Scott Margason, Kimberly Peticolas, and Mary Cirincione

Thank you to Claire, Allyssa, Brittany, and Natalie for the fantastic photoshoot. To my father-in-law and mother-in-law for your encouragement. To my brothers, Ryan and Matt, for being the most efficient taste-testers. To my parents for sponsoring so many products and for all your support. To my husband for always believing in me and supporting me no matter what. And to God for giving me the idea to write this book, and for giving me everything I need to succeed.

© 2017 Happy Mason Jar, LLC
All Rights Reserved.

Happy Mason Jar, LLC. 5 Palisades Drive. Albany, NY 12205.
www.happymasonjar.com.

ISBN: 978-0-692-91342-0

TABLE of CONTENTS

Brunch Treats

Party Time

Date Night

Cake Classics

Summer Sweets

Cozy Holidays

Dedicated to my best friend and husband, Devin Cremeans.
I love you with all my heart.

A LETTER from ALYSSA

HAPPINESS IS A POWERFUL FEELING.

It can be found in life's celebrations. It dwells in our most meaningful relationships. A moment of happiness can be activated with something as small as a hug, a smile, a gift, or a piece of cake.

Ever since I was a child, the smell of treats baking in the oven has always activated that feeling of happiness inside of me. Growing up in upstate New York, I remember dancing through apple orchards, picking fresh strawberries, and eating apple cider donuts at our local pumpkin patch. Those were all happy memories for me, mostly because they meant coming home and baking for hours with my mom.

It didn't take long for me to discover that baking was my favorite hobby. I loved coming up with new dessert recipes, concoctions, and "inventions," as I used to call them. My mom was such a good sport. I would make a huge mess in the kitchen, combining the strangest ingredients, and she would just laugh. I'm sure I seemed like a bad baker at the time, but my parents always believed in me and told me what an incredible baker I was.

I quickly grew into those words they spoke over me, and I learned what tastes good and what doesn't when it comes to baking. By fifth grade, I started my first baking business and gave all the proceeds to local nonprofits.

Since then, my palate has grown. I've lived abroad in Europe and traveled to more than a dozen countries, and now know how exhilarating it can be to taste the distinct flavors of the world.

I was intrigued by how my white cake recipe tasted so different when I made it in Guatemala, and by how delicious a bitter chocolate tart could taste in Germany.

I settled back home in upstate New York to become involved at my church and to marry Devin, the man of my dreams. Life was pretty amazing! I was a new wife. I was working full time in a high-capacity communications role. But there was something missing. I encountered a dilemma that men and women everywhere face: Baking was basically impossible with my busy lifestyle.

That's when I uncovered the hidden value of the American mason jar and its near-magical ability to be used as a serving dish, drinking glass, and storage container that will keep desserts fresh for days!

Upon my new discovery, my passion for food soon outgrew hobby status and I became focused on creating something to make people's lives just a little bit happier and a little bit easier.

The reason I wrote The Happy Mason Jar is to add a little relief to everyday life. These delicious desserts can be prepared in around thirty minutes, but stay fresh for over a week.

Thank you for inviting my book into your home. I hope these recipes add a little happiness to your life, just as they have to mine!

I wish you all the best. Happy baking!

Alyssa Marie Cremeans

THE PERFECT JAR FOR YOU

Mason jars come in all shapes and sizes. For pies, brownies, and meringues, the short jars make digging in much easier. For cakes and cheesecakes, the tall, wide-mouth jars show off the beautiful layers.

For jars that are baked in the oven, such as cheesecakes, brownies, or meringues, only use the 8-ounce mason jars. Changing the size of the jars can alter baking time significantly. Most recipes in this book call for short or tall 8-ounce mason jars. But for desserts baked prior to assembling the jars, such as cakes, feel free to use smaller or larger jars.

TALL 8-OZ   SHORT 8-OZ

16-OZ

For large 16-ounce jars, use half the number of mason jars the recipe calls for.

For more petite 4-ounce jars, use double the number of mason jars the recipe calls for.

4-OZ

NARROW MOUTH

Always use wide-mouth mason jars when you are baking mason jar cakes. Mason jars with narrow mouths can make layering very challenging. (See next page)

LAYERS 101

Layering a mason jar dessert is easier than you may think. Desserts such as cheesecakes, pies, or meringues can be layered prior to baking. Cake desserts can be layered and assembled after baking. Here is a step-by-step process to help you create cake layers in a mason jar.

Bake the cake in a 9 x 13-inch pan. Let the cake cool completely.

When the cake is cool, place a mason jar upside down on top of the cake.

Press the top of the mason jar into the cake, twisting if necessary, to create a clean, circular layer.

Gently pull the mason jar out of the cake. If the layer stays in the mason jar, gently remove it with your fingers.

Continue creating circular layers with the remainder of the cake. Set each layer aside.

Assemble each mason jar according to the recipe directions. Use the remaining chunks of cake to create layers, if needed.

BRUNCH TREATS

APPLESAUCE CRUMBLE CAKE

🕐 active prep: 20 min   🕐 inactive prep: 40 min   🕐 bake time: 35 to 40 min

CAKE

1½ cups applesauce (sweetened or unsweetened)

2 teaspoons baking soda

¾ cup sugar

¾ cup brown sugar

¾ cup shortening

2 cups flour

1 teaspoon ground cloves

1 teaspoon cinnamon

1 teaspoon ground allspice

¼ teaspoon salt

2 teaspoons vanilla extract

FROSTING

½ cup butter, room temperature

¾ cup brown sugar

¼ teaspoon salt

5 tablespoons milk

2 teaspoons vanilla extract

3 cups powdered sugar

Cinnamon sugar and/ or walnuts for garnish (optional)

Some of the best recipes are the ones that are passed down over generations. This recipe was my great-grandmother's, a Kansas native who baked ten to twelve desserts a day for her family's farmhands! When Devin and I were first married, my father-in-law was thrilled to discover I brought an applesauce cake recipe to the family since it's his favorite dessert and a family tradition. His grandmother used to make applesauce cake once each year for Thanksgiving brunch, and the family would salivate with excitement. Try out this recipe, and it may just become a family tradition for you, too!

• •

MAKES EIGHT TALL 8-OZ MASON JARS

1. Preheat your oven to 325°F. Spray a 9 x 13-inch pan with cooking spray.

2. In a medium bowl, stir together the applesauce and baking soda.

3. In another medium bowl, beat together the sugar, brown sugar, and shortening. Add the spices, salt, and vanilla to the sugar mixture, and beat until the batter is smooth.

4. Stir the applesauce mixture into the sugar mixture.

5. Spread the batter in the prepared 9 x 13-inch pan. Bake for 35 to 40 minutes, or until a toothpick inserted into the center comes out clean.

6. Allow the cake to cool completely, about 40 minutes.

7. In a large bowl, use a mixer to combine all the frosting ingredients together until completely smooth.

8. Using the rim of a mason jar, create layers from the cake. (See page 10)

9. Layer each mason jar with 1 layer of cake and 1 layer of frosting, followed by a second layer of cake and a second layer of frosting. Garnish with cinnamon sugar and/or walnuts (if desired).

10. These mason jar cakes taste best warm. To serve, remove the lids and heat each jar in the microwave, one at a time, for 20 seconds.

Pairing **Gewürztraminer**
Chateau St. Michelle

LEMON BAR IN A JAR

🕐 active prep: 10 min   🕐 inactive prep: 2 hours   🕐 bake time: 25 min

CRUST

1 cup crushed vanilla wafer cookies

2 tablespoons butter

LEMON FILLING

4 large eggs

¾ cup sugar

⅓ cup lemon juice

1 teaspoon lemon zest

2 tablespoons sweetened condensed milk

¼ cup flour

¼ teaspoon salt

TOPPING

1 cup whipped topping

6 fresh lemon wedges

Summer brunches, baby showers, and bridal showers are my favorite occasions for these sweet and light desserts. The bright yellow color of the filling and the white whipped topping add to any happy and celebratory atmosphere!

. . . .

MAKES SIX 4-OZ MASON JARS

1. Preheat your oven to 350°F.

2. Melt the butter in a microwave-safe bowl by heating it on high for 30 seconds. Drizzle it over the crushed vanilla wafer cookies, and stir until the cookies are evenly coated. Distribute the crust mixture evenly into each mason jar.

3. In a large bowl, whisk together all the ingredients for the lemon filling. Distribute the filling into each mason jar.

4. Fill a brownie pan with ½ inch of water and place the jars inside.

5. Bake the jars for 25 minutes until the filling starts to set. Remove the jars from the oven and allow them to cool for about 45 minutes.

6. When the jars have cooled completely, refrigerate them for at least 1 hour before serving. Garnish with whipped topping and lemon slices, if desired.

Pairing **Mario! The Sparkling Lemoncello**
Saraceni Wines

BLUEBERRY COFFEE CAKE

active prep: 25 min inactive prep: none bake time: 40 min

CAKE

1¼ cups sugar

½ cup butter, room temperature

3 large eggs

1¾ cups flour

1 teaspoon lemon juice

2 teaspoons baking powder

1 teaspoon salt

1 teaspoon vanilla extract

½ teaspoon almond extract

¾ cup milk

1 cup fresh blueberries

TOPPING

½ teaspoon cinnamon

⅓ cup chopped hazelnuts

½ cup sugar

¼ cup flour

Dash of salt

¼ cup cold butter

1 cup fresh blueberries

Chocolate chips (optional)

Every summer as a little girl, I would go blueberry picking in Vermont with my mom. One of the many reasons I loved it was because I had her all to myself, no little brothers around. I can still remember the smell of ripe blueberries kissing my face in the summer breeze. The entire ride home, my mom and I would dream of the endless possibilities we could make with our hard day's work . . . blueberry cobbler, blueberry pie, blueberry jelly, blueberry coffee cake. No one could make a coffee cake like my mom could. We would go home and bake with blueberries for hours until our fingers turned purple.

MAKES EIGHT SHORT 8-OZ MASON JARS

1. Preheat your oven to 350°F.
2. In a large bowl, beat together the sugar and butter.
3. Add all the remaining cake ingredients, except for the blueberries, mixing until the batter is smooth.
4. Fold in the blueberries.
5. Fill each mason jar just under halfway with batter.
6. For the topping, stir together the cinnamon, chopped hazelnuts, sugar, flour, salt, and chocolate chips.
7. Cut the butter into small pieces over the topping, and mash it together with a fork.
8. Distribute the topping into each mason jar.
9. Fill 1 or 2 pans with approximately 1 inch of water, and place the jars inside.
10. Bake the jars for about 40 minutes, or until a toothpick inserted into the center comes out clean. Top with fresh blueberries and chocolate chips, if desired.

Pairing **Peach Bellini**
Combine one part peach nectar with one part chilled prosecco

MANDARIN ORANGE CAKE

active prep: 10 min   inactive prep: 45 min   bake time: 25 to 30 min

CAKE

1 box (16.5 ounces) butter cake mix

1 can (11 ounces) mandarin oranges (undrained)

4 large eggs

½ cup oil

FROSTING

1 can (20 ounces) crushed pineapples (undrained)

1 box (3.25 ounces) instant vanilla pudding mix

1 container (12 ounces) whipped topping

One of my favorite things to do when baking is to re-create memories for the ones I love. When my dad was first married to my mom, she made him a mandarin orange cake, and it has been his favorite dessert ever since. For this recipe, I decided to use my mom's recipe to re-create my dad's all-time favorite. Not only does he love this cake, but it brings him back to the years when he and my mom were first married.

. . . .

MAKES EIGHT TALL 8-OZ MASON JARS

1. Preheat your oven to 350°F. Spray a 9 x 13-inch pan with cooking spray.
2. In a large bowl, combine all the cake ingredients until the batter is smooth.
3. Spread the batter into the prepared pan and bake for 25 to 30 minutes, or until a toothpick inserted into the center comes out clean. Allow the cake to cool for 45 minutes.
4. While the cake is cooling, whisk together all the frosting ingredients.
5. Create circular cake layers using the rim of a mason jar. (See page 10)
6. Place 1 layer of cake into each jar, followed by a thick layer of the frosting. Continue layering until the jars are filled to the brim.
7. Keep the jars refrigerated until you are ready to enjoy.

Pairing **Sauvignon Blanc**
Pomelo

BANANAS ADDICTION

🕐 active prep: 10 min   🕐 inactive prep: none   🕐 bake time: none

1 cup butter

½ cup sugar

½ cup packed light brown sugar

½ cup sweetened condensed milk

2 teaspoons vanilla extract

1 teaspoon ground cinnamon

¼ cup light rum (optional)

4 ripe bananas, diced into ½-inch slices

½ cup chopped walnuts (optional)

4 cups vanilla ice cream

The sweet aroma of cinnamon, rum, and brown sugar cooking on the stovetop always brings me back to my childhood. I'm reminded of my dad eating his favorite rum raisin ice cream on a crisp fall evening, while my mom pulls cinnamon apple strudel out of the oven. It was much later in life that I first discovered the addictive taste of a classic bananas foster dessert, and I have been in love with it ever since. But be warned: this dessert can get a little messy!

. . . .

MAKES EIGHT SHORT 8-OZ MASON JARS

1. In a medium-sized saucepan (cast iron is ideal), heat the butter on low heat until it melts.
2. Immediately add both the sugar and brown sugar, stirring slowly until the mixture is mostly smooth. Some of the butter may remain separated from the sugar.
3. Stir in the sweetened condensed milk, vanilla, cinnamon, and rum (if desired).
4. Increase the heat to medium-high, and stir constantly for about 3 minutes. Reduce the heat back to low, stirring for another 30 seconds.
5. Add the diced bananas and the chopped walnuts (if desired) to the sauce mixture.
6. Distribute the ice cream into each mason jar and top with the banana sauce.

If you would like to save your Bananas Addiction for later, distribute the banana sauce into each jar with no ice cream. Cover each jar with a lid and refrigerate when it is completely cooled. When you are ready to serve, remove the lid and heat the jars in the microwave on high for 30 seconds. Top with the ice cream and enjoy! Bananas Addiction is also delicious served over waffles and pancakes.

Pairing   **Chenin Blanc + Viognier Blend**
Pine Ridge

PARTY
TIME

NEW YORK, NEW YORK CHEESECAKE

active prep: 25 min   inactive prep: 1 hour 40 min   bake time: 30 min

The first time Devin and I went on a date in New York City, he took me to a fun diner in Times Square with the best cheesecake I'd ever tried. Devin would go on and on about how amazing their cheesecake was. If the way to a man's heart is truly through his belly, I knew I had to come up with a cheesecake recipe that he could call his new favorite. I'm proud to share with you that this cheesecake has done the trick! Maybe this recipe is truly the best, or maybe Devin just says that because I'm his wife. Either way, I'm pretty happy with the recipe!

CRUST LAYER

2 tablespoons butter

1 cup crushed graham crackers

CHEESECAKE LAYER

16 ounces cream cheese, room temperature

½ cup sweetened condensed milk

2 large eggs

2 tablespoons lemon juice

½ cup sugar

½ cup sour cream

¼ teaspoon salt

STRAWBERRY SAUCE

2 cups strawberries, quartered

3 tablespoons sugar

1 tablespoon lemon juice

2 teaspoons cornstarch

¼ cup water

Additional strawberries for garnish (optional)

MAKES SIX SHORT OR TALL 8-OZ MASON JARS

1. Preheat your oven to 300°F.

2. Melt the butter in a microwave-safe bowl by heating it on high for 30 seconds. Drizzle the butter over the crushed graham crackers, and stir until the graham crackers are evenly coated. Sprinkle the mixture into each mason jar. Do not press the graham crackers to the bottom of the jar, so as not to make it too firm.

3. In a large bowl, beat the cream cheese until it is smooth. Add the sweetened condensed milk, eggs, lemon juice, sugar, and sour cream. Continue beating until the batter is smooth.

4. Distribute the cheesecake batter into each mason jar, leaving about 1 inch of space at the top.

5. Fill a brownie pan with 1 inch of water and place the mason jars inside. Bake the mason jars for about 30 minutes, or until the cheesecakes begin to set.

6. When the cheesecakes are out of the oven, remove them from the water bath to allow them to cool for about 40 minutes. Then place the jars in the refrigerator and allow them to set for at least 1 hour.

7. While the cheesecakes are setting, combine all the ingredients for the strawberry sauce layer in a skillet over medium-high heat, stirring thoroughly.

8. When the sauce is simmering, immediately reduce the heat to low, stirring regularly so the sauce does not burn.

9. Continue allowing the sauce to cook until it is thickened. This should take about 5 minutes. Remove it from the heat and allow it to cool for about 30 minutes.

10. When the cheesecakes are set and the sauce is cool, top each cheese-cake with the strawberry sauce. Garnish with more strawberries, if desired. Keep the cheesecakes in your refrigerator until you are ready to enjoy!

Pairing **Scheurebe Kabinett**
Geil

RAINBOW SPRINKLE CAKE

🕐 active prep: 30 min   🕐 inactive prep: 40 min   🕐 bake time: 30 to 35 min

CAKE

1 cup butter, room temperature

2 cups sugar

3 large eggs

1 cup heavy cream

1 teaspoon vanilla extract

2 cups flour

1½ teaspoons baking powder

½ teaspoon salt

¼ cup rainbow sprinkles

FROSTING

1 cup butter, room temperature

3 cups powdered sugar

3 tablespoons sweetened condensed milk

1 tablespoon vanilla extract

Pink food coloring

Blue food coloring

Yellow food coloring

There's something about funfetti cake that tastes so much better than regular white cake. Maybe it's because of the old saying, "You eat with your eyes before you do with your mouth." The bright rainbow sprinkles and colorful frosting jump out of the jar to make your mouth water before even taking a bite. These mason jar Rainbow Sprinkle Cakes are great birthday party favors for adults and kids!

. . . .

MAKES EIGHT TALL 8-OZ MASON JARS

1. Preheat your oven to 350°F. Spray two 9-inch round cake pans thoroughly with nonstick baking spray.
2. Beat the butter and sugar together with an electric mixer until they become light and fluffy. Add the eggs, heavy cream, and vanilla.
3. In a separate bowl, stir together the flour, baking powder, and salt. While beating on low with an electric mixer, slowly add the dry ingredients to the wet ingredients until the batter is smooth. Stir in the sprinkles.
4. Spread the batter between the pans and place them into the oven. Bake for 30 to 35 minutes, or until a toothpick inserted into the center comes out clean.
5. Remove the cakes and allow them to cool completely, about 40 minutes.
6. For the frosting, beat together the butter, powdered sugar, sweetened condensed milk, and vanilla in a medium bowl until the mixture is smooth.
7. Divide the frosting into 3 separate small bowls. Add 1 color of food coloring to each bowl, stirring until each frosting is a solid color. The amount of food coloring you use depends on how deep you want the colors to be.
8. Combine all 3 frostings into a large bowl, gently folding together 4 to 5 times to create a rainbow effect.
9. To assemble the jars, create circular layers in the cake. (See page 10)
10. Place 1 layer of cake into each jar, followed by a large spoonful of frosting. Repeat this until the jars are filled to the brim.

Pairing **Rosé**
Saratoga Sparkling

LINDSAY'S CHOCOLATE SUNDAE CAKE

🕐 active prep: 10 min   🕐 inactive prep: 45 min   🕐 bake time: 25 min

CAKE LAYER

1 box (16 ounces) chocolate cake mix and required ingredients

TOPPING LAYER

1½ cups chocolate chips

1 cup sweetened condensed milk

1 cup caramel syrup (bottled or canned)

1 container (8 ounces) whipped topping

Maraschino cherries for garnish (optional)

I was so happy when I discovered my friend Lindsay loves to bake as much as I do. She is one of the most well-rounded people I know, always surprising me with her hobbies, skills, and knowledge on various topics. She once gave me her top secret chocolate cake recipe. The recipe was so easy to make, I almost felt guilty serving it! Lindsay agreed that this recipe had to be in my book. Thanks Lindsay!

. . . .

MAKES EIGHT TALL 8-OZ MASON JARS

1. Preheat your oven to 350°F.
2. In a large bowl, prepare the cake mix according to package directions.
3. Carefully fill ⅓ of each mason jar with cake batter. Do your best to not spill the batter on the sides of the jar.
4. Fill 1 or 2 baking pans with 1 inch of water. Place the mason jars inside and bake for 25 minutes, or until a knife inserted into the center comes out clean.
5. Carefully pull the baking pans out of the oven. Distribute ¾ cup of the chocolate chips into the mason jars and remove them from the water.
6. Allow the mason jars to cool completely, about 45 minutes.
7. While the cakes are cooling, spoon the whipped topping into a medium-sized bowl.
8. Pour the remaining ¾ cup of chocolate chips into a small microwave-safe bowl and heat in the microwave for 30 seconds. The chocolate chips will not be melted. Thoroughly stir them into the whipped topping to create a chunky whipped cream. Set aside.
9. When the cakes are cool, poke them each 3 to 4 times with a fork.
10. Coat each cake evenly with the sweetened condensed milk and the caramel topping.
11. Top the cakes with the whipped topping and garnish with cherries (if desired).

Pairing **Splendia Fragolino**
Saraceni Wines

CHOCOLATE PEANUT BUTTER PIE

🕐 active prep: 20 min   🕐 inactive prep: 45 min   🕐 bake time: 25 to 30 min

1 box (14.5 ounces) brownie mix and required ingredients

1 cup peanut butter

1 cup powdered sugar

1½ cups heavy cream

8 ounces whipped topping

¼ teaspoon salt

One of the first desserts I ever made as a kid was a no-bake peanut butter pie. Instantly, I discovered it was a true crowd-pleaser. Just like this dessert, it was so quick and easy to make. If you ever struggle with deciding what kind of dessert to make—whether it's a romantic evening or a family picnic—this is a perfect go-to!

• •

MAKES EIGHT TALL 8-OZ MASON JARS

1. Bake the brownies according to package directions. Allow them to cool completely, about 45 minutes.
2. In a large bowl, combine the peanut butter and powdered sugar. Slowly add the heavy cream, beating on the lowest setting.
3. When the heavy cream is added, turn the mixer up to the highest setting and beat for 1 to 2 minutes, or until soft peaks begin to form. Fold in the whipped topping.
4. Refrigerate the peanut butter batter until you are ready to use it.
5. When the brownies are cool, break them into bite-sized pieces, about 1-inch thick.
6. Layer half the brownie chunks along the bottom of each mason jar, pushing them down gently to avoid air pockets.
7. Distribute half the peanut butter batter into each mason jar.
8. Distribute the remaining brownie chunks, followed by the peanut butter batter into each mason jar.
9. Refrigerate the desserts until you are ready to serve.

Pairing **Chocolate Red Wine**
Chocolate Shop Wines

MINT PATTY BROWNIES

🕐 active prep: 20 min   🕐 inactive prep: 15 min   🕐 bake time: 45 min

BROWNIES

¾ cup butter, room temperature

1½ cups sugar

3 large eggs

1 teaspoon vanilla extract

⅔ cup cocoa powder

½ teaspoon baking powder

¼ teaspoon salt

¾ cup flour

8 peppermint patties

FROSTING

½ cup butter, room temperature

2 cups powdered sugar

½ teaspoon mint extract

¼ teaspoon green food coloring

As the brownies bake, the patties melt and spread throughout the brownie so you get a delicious burst of mint with each bite. These make delicious favors for St. Patrick's Day parties—or any party for that matter.

. . . .

MAKES EIGHT SHORT 8-OZ MASON JARS

1. Preheat your oven to 350°F. Spray the inside of each mason jar with cooking spray.

2. Place the butter in a large bowl. Using a hand-mixer, add the sugar, eggs, vanilla, cocoa powder, baking powder, and salt.

3. Add the flour, mixing until the batter is smooth. Evenly distribute the brownie batter into each mason jar, filling halfway.

4. Place a peppermint patty into the center of each jar. Place the mason jars into pans filled with 1 inch of water. Bake for 45 minutes.

5. Allow the brownies to cool for 15 minutes before frosting.

6. For the frosting, combine the butter, powdered sugar, mint extract, and green food coloring in a bowl, beating until the frosting is smooth.

7. Distribute the frosting on top of the brownies and serve!

Pairing **Australian Shiraz**
Layer Cake Wines

DATE
NIGHT

MIDNIGHT RASPBERRY CAKE

🕐 active prep: 30 min   🕐 inactive prep: 15 min   🕐 bake time: 35 min

CAKE

¾ cup butter, room temperature

1½ cups sugar

4 ounces semisweet baking chocolate

⅔ cup heavy cream

3 large eggs

1 teaspoon vanilla

2 cups flour

1 teaspoon salt

1 teaspoon baking soda

1 teaspoon baking powder

½ cup cocoa powder

BERRY GLAZE

½ cup butter

2 cups frozen raspberries (or mixed berries), slightly thawed

1 cup sugar

EXTRA

1 cup chocolate syrup

Dark chocolate mixed with raspberry—I wish I could meet the person who came up with such a brilliant combination. The rich undertones in dark chocolate are a perfect complement to the sweet, tart flavors in the fruit. The only party who can third-wheel such a masterpiece is the sweet fizzy refreshment: Rosa Regale.

· ·

MAKES EIGHT TALL 8-OZ MASON JARS

1. Preheat your oven to 325°F. Spray a 9 x 13-inch pan with cooking spray.
2. Mix the butter and sugar in a large bowl.
3. In a microwave-safe bowl, heat the baking chocolate and heavy cream together for 30 seconds and stir. Continue heating for 15 seconds at a time, stirring between each cycle, until the chocolate is melted.
4. Combine melted chocolate with butter and sugar mixture, and beat while adding the eggs and vanilla.
5. In a medium bowl, stir together the dry ingredients. Add the dry ingredients to the wet ingredients, beating until the batter is smooth.
6. Spread the batter into the prepared baking pan and bake for about 35 minutes, or until a toothpick inserted into the center comes out clean. Allow the cake to cool for at least 15 minutes.
7. Heat ½ cup of butter, 2 cups of frozen raspberries, and 1 cup of sugar over medium heat. Stir thoroughly until the ingredients are combined well and the butter is melted. Press the berries with a spoon to remove extra juice.
8. Reduce the heat to low for 5 minutes. Using a strainer, pour the mixture into a bowl to remove the seeds.
9. Once the cake is slightly cooled, create circular slices in the cake using the rim of a mason jar. (See page 10)
10. Distribute a slice into each jar and top with a spoonful of the berry glaze and a spoonful of chocolate syrup. Repeat until the jars are full.

Pairing **Sparkling Red**
Rosa Regale

HAZELNUT TIRAMISU

🕐 active prep: 20 min   🕐 inactive prep: 1 hour   🕐 bake time: according to package directions

TIRAMISU

1 package white cake mix and required ingredients

¼ cup sweetened condensed milk

¾ cup chocolate hazelnut spread

¼ cup espresso

FROSTING

½ cup heavy cream

2 tablespoons butter, room temperature

1 cup powdered sugar

½ teaspoon vanilla extract

When I was a little girl, tiramisu was always something the grown-ups had for dessert. It was off-limits to my brothers and me, probably because there was espresso and we certainly didn't need that! To reclaim the tiramisu I dreamed of eating in my childhood, I invented my own version with one of the world's most favorite ingredients: chocolate hazelnut spread. Although this version of tiramisu is not caffeinefree, it's easy and tasty!

. . . .

MAKES EIGHT TALL 8-OZ MASON JARS

1. Bake the white cake according to package directions in a 9 x 13-inch pan.

2. Allow the cake to cool for about 30 minutes.

3. Using the rim of a mason jar, create layers in the cake. (See page 10)

4. Place 1 layer of the cake into each mason jar and poke holes using a fork.

5. Distribute and drizzle the sweetened condensed milk into each mason jar.

6. Using a microwave-safe bowl, heat the chocolate hazelnut spread in the microwave for 30 seconds and stir. Distribute a spoonful of the warm spread into each jar.

7. Distribute another layer of the cake into each mason jar. If there are not enough cake layers, use the remaining cake crumbs.

8. Drizzle the espresso into each jar.

9. In a medium bowl, combine the heavy cream, butter, powdered sugar, and vanilla. Beat with a mixer until stiff peaks form.

10. Distribute the frosting into each mason jar, spreading evenly over the tiramisu layer.

11. Garnish each mason jar with the white chocolate chips and chocolate shavings (if desired).

12. Refrigerate for 30 minutes before serving.

Pairing **East India Solera Sherry**
Emilio Lustau

OREO DE MENTHE CHEESECAKE

🕐 active prep: 5 min   🕐 inactive prep: 1 hour 45 min   🕐 bake time: 30 to 35 min

OREO LAYER

¼ cup butter

2 cups crushed oreos

MINT LAYER

12 ounces cream cheese, room temperature

¾ cup sugar

2 large eggs

¼ cup crème de menthe liqueur

Bethany Marcelle has been my best girlfriend since the third grade. When you become best friends with an Italian, you gain a second family. Suddenly, I had four more siblings and two more parents who always seemed to feed me the most amazing yummies. One year, Bethany's mom, Diane, made a chocolate mint cake for Bethany's birthday and it was love at first bite. I never knew that two flavors could taste so delicious together. Since then, I have become partial to all desserts with chocolate mint.

. . . .

MAKES SIX TALL 8-OZ MASON JARS

1. Preheat your oven to 300°F.

2. Melt the butter in a microwave-safe bowl by heating it on high for 30 seconds. Drizzle it over the oreos, and stir until the oreos are evenly coated. Set aside.

3. In a large bowl, use a mixer to combine the cream cheese and sugar. Slowly add the eggs and liqueur. Continue beating until the batter is smooth.

4. To assemble the mason jars, take half the mint batter and distribute evenly into each jar. Distribute 1 cup of the oreo mixture among the jars. Repeat each layer again.

5. Fill a brownie pan with 1 inch of water and place the jars inside. Bake the jars in the bath for 30 to 35 minutes.

6. When the cheesecakes are finished baking, remove them from the bath and allow them to cool for 45 minutes. Place them in the refrigerator and allow them to set for 1 hour. Garnish with crushed oreos, if desired.

Pairing **Scheurebe Kabinett**
Geil

CHOCOLATE HAZELNUT CAKE

🕐 active prep 10 min 🕐 inactive prep: 30 min 🕐 bake time: 30 to 35 min

CAKE

6 tablespoons butter, room temperature

1½ cups sugar

1 cup semisweet chocolate chips

¾ cup buttermilk

1½ tablespoons black coffee

1½ teaspoons vanilla

2 large eggs

¾ teaspoon salt

1⅓ cups cake flour

6 tablespoons cocoa powder

¾ teaspoon baking powder

1½ teaspoons baking soda

FROSTING LAYER

¼ cup butter, room temperature

1 cup chocolate hazelnut spread

⅔ cup heavy cream

¼ cup powdered sugar

Your guests will be in heaven with this dessert. My husband has a huge sweet tooth. His love for desserts was quite convenient for me when testing these recipes. Out of all thirty recipes, he declared that this is his favorite dessert in the book, and he doesn't use his words lightly!

· ·

MAKES SIX TALL 8-OZ MASON JARS

1. Preheat your oven to 350°F. Spray a 9 x 13-inch pan with cooking spray.
2. In a large bowl, beat the butter and sugar until they are well-combined.
3. Place the chocolate chips in a small, microwave-safe bowl and heat on high for 30 seconds. Remove them from the microwave and stir. Return the chocolate chips to the microwave for 15 seconds at a time, stirring in between each cycle until they are fully melted.
4. Beat the melted chocolate chips into the butter-and-sugar mixture. Add the remaining cake ingredients, and mix until the batter becomes smooth and fluffy. This should take 30 seconds or less.
5. Spread the batter evenly across the cake pan. Bake for 30 to 35 minutes, or until a toothpick inserted into the center comes out clean.
6. Remove the cake from the oven and allow it to cool for 30 minutes.
7. While the cake is cooling, combine all the frosting ingredients in a large bowl. Beat the ingredients on high for 1 to 2 minutes, or until soft, creamy peaks begin to form.
8. To assemble the mason jars, break the cake into 2 to 3-inch chunks.
9. Distribute half of the cake chunks into the mason jars, gently pushing the cake to the bottom of the jar to avoid large air pockets. Distribute half the chocolate hazelnut frosting into the jars.
10. For the second cake layer, distribute the remaining half of cake chunks into each mason jar, topping with the remaining frosting.

Pairing **Lambrusco**
Riunite

CREAMY KEY LIME PIE

🕐 active prep: 15 min   🕐 inactive prep: none   🕐 bake time: none

CRUST

4 cups vanilla wafer
cookies

½ cup butter

FILLING

1 cup mascarpone
cheese

1 cup sugar

2 cups heavy cream

2 teaspoons vanilla

2 tablespoons lime
juice (about 3 limes)

2 tablespoons lime
zest (about 3 limes)

½ teaspoon salt

TOPPING

Lime peel for garnish
(optional)

If you're a spontaneous party host, these are some great ingredients to have around your house. This dessert has no bake or setting time and takes only 15 minutes to make so it can be enjoyed immediately. The sweet lime flavors are mild enough to please just about any palate!

• •

MAKES EIGHT 4-OZ MASON JARS

1. Place the vanilla wafer cookies in a large plastic bag, and crush them into small pieces.

2. Melt the butter in a microwave-safe bowl by heating it on high for 30 seconds. Drizzle it over the vanilla wafer cookies, and stir until the cookies are evenly coated. Set aside.

3. Distribute half the cookie mixture into the mason jars. Set aside the remaining cookie mixture.

4. In a large bowl, use a mixer to beat the mascarpone cheese while slowly adding the sugar. Mixing on low, slowly add the heavy cream, vanilla, lime juice, lime zest, and salt until it is mostly combined. Then turn the mixer to high until stiff peaks begin to form.

5. Distribute half of the filling mixture into the mason jars. Add the remaining crumb mixture into each jar. For the final layer, add the remaining filling mixture into each jar, followed by the lime peel, if desired. Refrigerate until you're ready to serve!

Pairing **Sauvignon Blanc**
Kono Pure Taste of New Zealand

CAKE CLASSICS

BLUEBERRY ALMOND VELVET CAKE

active prep: 30 min   inactive prep: 40 min   bake time: 30 to 35 min

CAKE

1 cup butter, room temperature

2 cups sugar

3 large eggs

2 cups flour

1½ teaspoons baking powder

½ teaspoon salt

1 cup heavy cream

1 tablespoon vanilla extract

1½ teaspoons neon blue food coloring

FROSTING

1 cup butter, room temperature

4 cups powdered sugar

3 tablespoons sweetened condensed milk

½ teaspoon almond extract

½ cup crushed blueberries

3 drops purple food coloring (optional)

Red velvet cake is one of our family favorites. Whenever I discover a dessert my family loves, I'm always looking for ways to mix it up and make a different version of it! I took a social media survey to find out what colors (other than red) would look appetizing as a "velvet cake." Most suggested blue or purple. Blueberry was the first flavor that popped into my mind, because it has a blue outside and purple inside. And, of course, almond tastes deliciously perfect when paired with blueberry.

. . . .

MAKES EIGHT TALL 8-OZ MASON JARS

1. Preheat your oven to 350°F. Spray a 9 x 13-inch pan with cooking spray.
2. In a large bowl, combine all the cake ingredients, except the food coloring. Beat until the batter becomes smooth.
3. Mix in the neon blue food coloring until the batter is a solid blue.
4. Spread the batter into the cake pan. Bake for 30 to 35 minutes, or until a toothpick inserted into the center comes out clean.
5. Remove the cake and allow it to cool completely, about 40 minutes.
6. For the frosting, use a hand-mixer to cream together the butter and powdered sugar. Add the sweetened condensed milk and almond extract, beating until the frosting is smooth.
7. Gently stir in the crushed blueberries and purple food coloring (if desired). Be sure not to stir more than necessary.
8. To assemble the mason jars, use the top of a jar to create circular layers. (See page 10)
9. Place 1 layer of cake into each jar, followed by a large spoonful of frosting. Repeat this until the jars are filled to the brim.
10 Keep the jars refrigerated or store them at room temperature.

Pairing **Moscato**
Stella

46

DEATH BY CARROTS

🕐 active prep: 30 min 🕐 inactive prep: 40 min 🕐 bake time: 35 to 40 min

CAKE

1½ sticks butter, room temperature

2 cups sugar

4 large eggs

1 cup vegetable oil

½ teaspoon almond extract

1 teaspoon lemon juice

2 cups cake flour

2 teaspoons baking soda

2 teaspoons ground cinnamon

1½ teaspoons salt

½ teaspoon baking powder

2 cups finely grated carrots

FROSTING

16 oz cream cheese, room temperature

½ cup butter, room temperature

1 teaspoon vanilla extract

3½ cups powdered sugar

One of the things I love most about carrot cake is its potential for diversity. Some people like to add walnuts, some like to add raisins. Some like to put grated carrots in the frosting, while others go as far as adding pineapple! This recipe is tried and true, but feel free to make it your own. Experiment and have fun, because that's what baking is all about.

. . . .

MAKES EIGHT TALL 8-OZ MASON JARS

1. Preheat your oven to 350°F. Spray a 9 x 13-inch pan with cooking spray.

2. In a large bowl, use a mixer to combine the butter and sugar. Add the eggs, vegetable oil, almond extract, and lemon juice, beating until the batter is smooth.

3. In a medium bowl, stir together the dry ingredients.

4. Slowly add the dry ingredients to the wet ingredients, beating on low with a mixer until the batter is smooth. Stir the grated carrots into the batter.

5. Spread the batter into the greased baking pan. Bake for 35 to 40 minutes, or until a toothpick inserted into the center comes out clean. Allow the cake to cool for about 40 minutes.

6. For the frosting, beat the cream cheese, butter, and vanilla together in a large bowl. Slowly add the powdered sugar, beating until the frosting is smooth.

7. When the cake is cool, create circular layers using the rim of a mason jar. (See page 10)

8. Distribute 1 layer into each mason jar followed by a spoonful of frosting. Repeat this for each layer until the mason jars are filled to the brim. Enjoy!

Pairing **Moscato d'Asti**
Scagliola Primo Bacio

HEAVEN'S COCONUT CAKE

🕐 active prep: 10 min 🕐 inactive prep: 30 min 🕐 bake time: 45 min

CAKE

1 box (16.25 ounces) white cake mix

3 egg whites

¼ cup oil

1 cup coconut milk

1 teaspoon coconut extract

1 cup shredded coconut

FROSTING

2 cups heavy cream

½ cup sugar

½ teaspoon lemon extract

½ teaspoon vanilla extract

If you're familiar with the other recipes in my cookbook, I'll have you know this one is quite unique from the rest. I'm a lover of decadent, almost overwhelmingly rich and filling desserts. But sometimes we need something a bit lighter. If you're having a day when you don't want something too heavy or if your palate generally favors a softer, simpler treat, opt for the light-and-satisfying flavors of Heaven's Coconut Cake with a chilled glass of prosecco. You can't go wrong.

• •

MAKES EIGHT TALL 8-OZ MASON JARS

1. Preheat your oven to 350°F. Spray a 9 x 13-inch pan with cooking spray.

2. In a large bowl, combine the cake mix, egg whites, oil, coconut milk, coconut extract, and 1 cup of shredded coconut.

3. Using a mixer, beat the ingredients until the batter becomes smooth. Spread the batter into the greased baking pan and bake for 30 minutes, or until a toothpick inserted into the center comes out clean. Allow the cake to cool completely, about 45 minutes.

4. For the whipped frosting, combine the remaining 1 cup of coconut, the heavy cream, and sugar in a large bowl. Add the lemon and vanilla extracts. Beat the batter on the mixer's low setting for 3 to 4 minutes, or until stiff peaks begin to form.

5. Create circular slices in the cake using the rim of a jar. (See page 10)

6. Distribute 1 slice of cake into each mason jar and top with a spoonful of whipped frosting. Repeat this for each layer until the mason jars are filled to the brim. Use the remaining chunks of cake to create additional cake layers, if necessary. Garnish with shredded coconut, if desired.

Pairing **Prosecco**
Saraceni Wines

GERMAN CHOCOLATE CAKE

⏱ active prep: 25 min   ⏱ inactive prep: 40 min   ⏱ bake time: according to package directions

1 package German chocolate cake mix and required ingredients

½ cup butter

1 cup evaporated milk

1 cup sugar

¼ cup mayonnaise

1 teaspoon vanilla

1½ cups coconut

1 cup pecans

I am a third-generation German-American, and my Oma used to bake the most delicious kuchen (cake)—German chocolate being one of them! Oma's desserts always tasted better to me than anyone else's because I knew the kind of woman my Oma was. Her desserts were made with strong, resilient hands. My Oma and Opa escaped Germany right before the Nazis came into power. They saw what was happening in their beloved country, and they refused to be a part of it. They came to America with less than twenty dollars in their pockets, speaking no English. If they hadn't had the courage to come to a foreign country with so little, I wouldn't be alive today. Although I was young when I knew my Oma, I was always in awe of her loving strength. She was the hardest worker I knew, but she still made time to show tremendous love to her family.

. . . .

MAKES EIGHT 8-OZ MASON JARS

1. Bake the German chocolate cake in a 9 x 13-inch pan according to package directions.
2. In a large saucepan, melt together the butter, evaporated milk, sugar, and mayonnaise over medium heat. Cook and stir until the mixture is slightly thickened, about 8 to 10 minutes.
3. Remove the mixture from the heat and immediately add the vanilla, coconut, and pecans, stirring thoroughly. Set aside to cool.
4. When the cake has cooled for about 40 minutes, create layers using the rim of a mason jar. (See page 10)
5. Place 1 layer in each mason jar and drizzle with a spoonful of frosting. Place a second layer in each jar and drizzle with the remaining frosting. If there are not enough cake layers, you can use the remaining crumbs to create layers.

Pairing **Red Sangria**
Mija

RED VELVET DECADENCE

🕐 active prep: 10 min 　　🕐 inactive prep: 45 min 　　🕐 bake time: 50 to 55 min

CAKE

2 cups sugar

1 cup butter, room temperature

⅓ cup canola oil

⅓ cup sweetened condensed milk

3 large eggs

½ cup chocolate milk

2 tablespoons plus 1 teaspoon liquid red food coloring

2 teaspoons vinegar

2½ cups flour

1 teaspoon salt

1 teaspoon baking soda

½ teaspoon baking powder

FROSTING

8 ounces cream cheese, room temperature

2 teaspoons vanilla extract

2 cups powdered sugar

3 tablespoons sweetened condensed milk

TOPPING

½ cup white chocolate chips (optional)

My senior year at Wheaton College in Illinois, I lived in a townhouse full of girls who grew up in the south. Born and raised in New York, the extroverted side of me soon grew to adore the southern culture of hospitality. One of my roommates baked sweets for house guests at all hours of the day, filling our home with delicious aromas. One evening, I noticed beautiful red velvet cakes in mason jars sitting on the ledge of our kitchen. Thinking they were available to anyone, I dove into one of the desserts. I was instantly lost in the addictive flavors, only to realize I robbed my roommate of a birthday gift she made for her friend! She was extremely gracious and forgiving, but I still felt so bad. I quickly learned how to make my own version of Red Velvet Decadence to make up for my mistake, and have been making red velvet cake in mason jars ever since!

• •

MAKES SIX TALL 8-OZ MASON JARS

1. Preheat your oven to 325°F. Spray a 9 x 13-inch pan with cooking spray.

2. In a large bowl, use a mixer to combine the sugar and butter. Add the remaining liquid ingredients and beat until the batter is smooth.

3. In a separate medium-sized bowl, stir together the dry cake ingredients. Fold the dry ingredients into the wet ingredients. Beat the batter on low speed with a mixer for 10 seconds or so to assure the batter is mixed well.

4. Spread the batter into the cake pan. Bake for 50 to 55 minutes, or until a toothpick inserted into the center comes out clean. When the cake is finished, remove it from the oven and allow it to cool for about 45 minutes. Don't be concerned if the cake dips slightly in the middle.

5. While the cake is cooling, use a mixer to combine all the frosting ingredients, and beat until it is completely smooth.

6. Create circular slices in the cake using the rim of a jar. (See page 10)

7. Distribute 1 slice into each mason jar and top with a spoonful of frosting. Repeat this for each layer until the mason jars are filled to the brim.

8. Sprinkle the white chocolate chips on top (if using). Enjoy!

Pairing **Sweet Rosé**
Castello del Poggio

SUMMER
SWEETS

DOS LECHES CAKE

active prep: 15 min   inactive prep: 45 min   bake time: 30 to 35 min

CAKE

4 large eggs

1 cup sugar

¼ cup heavy cream

1 teaspoon baking powder

¼ teaspoon salt

2 teaspoons vanilla extract

1 cup flour

MILK & CARAMEL

1 can (14 ounces sweetened condensed milk)

1 can (12 ounces) evaporated milk

¼ cup caramel syrup

TOPPING

1 cup heavy cream

¼ cup sugar

1 teaspoon vanilla extract

1 cup blueberries

1 cup maraschino cherries, drained and sliced in half

My mother makes a massive Tres Leches Cake every Fourth of July and it's one of my favorite desserts. Spanish for "Three Milks," Tres Leches is made with sweetened condensed milk, evaporated milk, and whole milk. But I always found two dilemmas with this cake: Its tremendous moisture made it difficult to serve, and I never saw the value of the whole milk. Enclosing the cake inside mason jars solves the moisture challenge. And the rich flavors of the sweetened condensed and evaporated milks are a strong enough team to stand on their own.

· ·

MAKES SIX TALL 8-OZ MASON JARS

1. Preheat your oven to 350°F. Spray a 9 x 13-inch pan with cooking spray.

2. In a large bowl, use a mixer to beat the eggs, sugar, and heavy cream together on high for 1 to 2 minutes, or until the batter becomes slightly fluffy.

3. Stir in the baking powder, salt, vanilla, and flour.

4. Spread the batter into the prepared pan. Bake for 35 to 40 minutes, or until a toothpick inserted into the center comes out clean.

5. While the cake bakes, whisk together the sweetened condensed milk, evaporated milk, and caramel. Set aside.

6. In a medium bowl, beat the ingredients for the topping (except for the blueberries and cherries) on high for 1 to 2 minutes, or until stiff peaks begin to form.

7. Once the cake is cool, make layers using the rim of a jar. (See age 10.)

8. To assemble each mason jar, distribute 1 layer of cake into each jar. Distribute half the milk mixture among the jars. Distribute half the blueberries and half the cherries among the jars, followed by half the whipped topping.

9. Repeat these layers with a second layer of cake (using chunks or crumbs, (if needed), followed by the remaining milk, berries, and whipped topping.

10. Keep the jars refrigerated until you are ready to enjoy.

Pairing **Moscato**
Bartenura

CREAMSICLE SHERBET

🕐 active prep: 5 min   🕐 inactive prep: 30 min   🕐 bake time: none

2 cups vanilla ice cream

3 cups orange soda

1 can (14 ounces) sweetened condensed milk

1 can (20 ounces) crushed pineapple

Try this on a hot day and you'll be glad you did! My little brothers, Ryan and Matt (who are no longer little!), have always loved creamsicle ice cream and this is one of their favorites. They enjoy this treat as a milkshake—served immediately with a straw and a spoon. I personally like it frozen for just 30 minutes!

. . . .

MAKES EIGHT TALL 8-OZ MASON JARS

1. Using a large microwave-safe bowl, heat the ice cream in the microwave for 1 minute.

2. In a large bowl, combine the orange soda, sweetened condensed milk, and crushed pineapple. Stir the mixture thoroughly.

3. Fill each mason jar ⅔ of the way with the orange soda mixture.

4. Fill the remainder of the jar with the partially melted ice cream.

5. Serve immediately as milkshakes, or place in the freezer for at least 30 minutes to serve as sherbet.

Pairing   **Blumond**
Saraceni Wines

COOKIE DOUGH BROWNIE SUNDAE

active prep: 10 min   inactive prep: 25 min   bake time: 35 to 40 min

BROWNIE LAYER

¾ cup butter, room temperature

1½ cups sugar

3 large eggs

1 teaspoon vanilla extract

⅔ cup cocoa powder

½ teaspoon baking powder

¼ teaspoon salt

¾ cup flour

COOKIE LAYER

1 roll (16.5 ounces) cookie dough

FOR SERVING

2 cups vanilla ice cream

Chocolate syrup (optional)

Caramel syrup (optional)

One evening when Devin and I were first married, I decided to surprise him with a combination of his favorite treats: cookie dough, brownies, and ice cream. He finished the entire dessert in less than five minutes! Since then, it's become a staple at our dinner parties.

. . . .

MAKES EIGHT SHORT 8-OZ MASON JARS

1. Preheat your oven to 350°F. Lightly spray the inside of each mason jar with cooking spray.

2. In a large bowl, use a mixer to combine the butter, sugar, eggs, vanilla, cocoa powder, baking powder, and salt.

3. Add the flour, beating until the brownie batter is smooth.

4. Spoon the brownie batter evenly into each mason jar. Fill 1 or 2 pans with ½ inch of water and place the mason jars inside. Bake for 15 minutes.

5. While the brownies are baking, separate the roll of cookie dough into 8 pieces.

6. Immediately after removing the brownies from the oven, place a piece of cookie dough into each mason jar. Be careful—the jars will be hot. Give the dough pieces a gentle push so they sink into the warm brownies.

7. Return the mason jars to the oven and allow them to bake for another 20 to 25 minutes.

8. When the brownies are done baking, let them cool for 25 minutes.

9. Top the brownies with the ice cream. Drizzle with the chocolate syrup and caramel syrup (if desired), and serve immediately.

To save for later: *Allow the mason jars to cool completely, approximately 1 hour, then seal them with their lids. When you are ready to serve, remove the lids and heat the jars in the microwave on high, one at a time, for 30 seconds each. Spoon the ice cream into each mason jar and drizzle with the optional chocolate and caramel syrups!*

Pairing **Sweet Red**
Castello del Poggio

GRAPEFRUIT MERINGUE PIE

🕐 active prep: 30 min　　🕐 inactive prep:1 hour　　🕐 bake time: 8 min

FILLING

1 cup sugar

3 tablespoons flour

2 tablespoons corn-starch

½ teaspoon salt

1½ cups water

Zest and juice of 1 grapefruit

Zest of 1 lemon

2 tablespoons butter

4 egg yolks

1 teaspoon pink food coloring (optional)

MERINGUE

4 egg whites

5 tablespoons sugar

CRUST

2 cups crushed lemon oreo cookies

From the time I was two years old until I went off to college, I grew up in a cozy corner of town next to the kindest neighbors. Warren and Annette became like another set of grandparents to my brothers and me. Every summer, we would salivate with anticipation as Warren would surprise us with fresh lemon meringue pies! How could a dessert so perfect be confined to just one citrus fruit? I had to explore more flavors of meringue, and that's how I came up with Grapefruit Meringue Pie!

. . . .

MAKES EIGHT SHORT 8-OZ MASON JARS

1. Preheat your oven to 350°F.
2. To make the grapefruit filling, squeeze the juice of the grapefruit over a strainer to remove any seeds. Whisk together the sugar, flour, corn-starch, salt, water, grapefruit juice, grapefruit zest, and lemon zest in a medium saucepan on medium-high heat.
3. Bring the mixture to a boil, stirring quickly. Stir in the butter until it melts. Reduce the heat to low.
4. Saving the egg whites for later, quickly beat the egg yolks with a mixer in a large heat-safe bowl. While beating the egg yolks, slowly add the hot mixture from the saucepan. Continue beating thoroughly on high until the hot mixture is added completely. Add the food coloring (if desired).
5. Return the mixture to the saucepan and continue to heat on low.
6. In a dry, clean bowl, make the meringue by using a whisk attachment to beat the egg whites on high until they become foamy.
7. Slowly add the sugar to the egg whites until soft peaks begin to form.
8. Distribute the crushed cookies on the bottom of each jar, followed by the grapefruit filling, topped with the meringue.
9. Fill a brownie pan with 1 inch of water. Place the jars inside and bake in the oven for 8 minutes, or until the meringue becomes lightly browned.
10. Let the jars cool completely, then refrigerate for an hour before serving.

Pairing **Volare**
Saraceni Wines

STRAWBERRY SHORTCAKE PARFAIT

🕐 active prep: 15 min 🕐 inactive prep: none 🕐 bake time: none

2 cups vanilla wafer cookies

¼ cup cream cheese, room temperature

¼ cup crushed walnuts

¼ cup sugar

1 cup vanilla ice cream

1 cup strawberry or raspberry sorbet

Strawberries for garnish (optional)

Do you remember the adrenaline rush you had as a child when the sound of the ice cream truck faintly moved closer and closer to you? I know I do! I remember the hot summer days in upstate New York when my little brothers and I would race out the front door to the street before my mom even gave us permission. Hopefully, we would look cute enough jumping up and down at the end of the driveway for her to agree to buy us ice cream. My mouth would water as I awaited my all-time favorite strawberry shortcake pop! I hope these easy, fun, Strawberry Shortcake Parfaits take you on a journey back to those hot summer days in your childhood when you raced your way to the ice cream truck.

· ·

MAKES EIGHT 4-OZ MASON JARS

1. Place the vanilla wafer cookies in a large bag. Crush them using a metal utensil until they are ½-inch pieces or smaller.

2. In a large bowl, beat the cream cheese, crushed vanilla wafer cookies, crushed walnuts, and sugar until they turn into a chunky crumble.

3. Distribute 1 cup of vanilla ice cream into the mason jars.

4. Distribute the crumble mixture into each of the jars.

5. Add the sorbet into each jar.

6. Keep the desserts in the freezer until you are ready to serve. If they are frozen for more than an hour before, allow them to thaw for 20 minutes.

7. Garnish with the strawberries (if using). Enjoy!

Pairing **White Sangria**
Mija

COZY HOLIDAYS

PUMPKIN SPICE CAKE

🕐 active prep: 10 min   🕐 inactive prep: 40 min   🕐 bake time: 25 min

CAKE

3 cups pancake mix

1 can (15 ounces) pumpkin

2 large eggs

1 cup oil

½ cup sugar

1 teaspoon vanilla

1 teaspoon cinnamon

1 teaspoon pumpkin pie spice

Cinnamon sugar (optional)

FROSTING

8 ounces cream cheese, room temperature

1 tablespoon vanilla extract

3 cups powdered sugar

My dear friend Claire is one of my favorite people. She's always there to build you up, and you'll always feel better even after spending just five minutes with her! This recipe was one of the first I created for this book and she happened to be at my house the day after I made it. We took our first bite and we instantly knew it was a winner. Once you start eating this dessert, you may find it very hard to stop!

. . . .

MAKES EIGHT TALL 8-OZ MASON JARS

1. Preheat your oven to 325°F. Spray a 9 x 13-inch pan with cooking spray.

2. In a large bowl, use a mixer to combine all the cake ingredients, except the cinnamon sugar.

3. Beat the mixture on high until the batter is smooth.

4. Spread the batter into the 9 x 13-inch pan and bake for 25 minutes, or until a toothpick inserted into the center comes out clean.

5. When the cake is done baking, allow it to cool for at least 40 minutes.

6. For the frosting, use a mixer to combine the cream cheese and vanilla. Slowly add the powdered sugar, mixing until the frosting is smooth. The frosting will be very thick.

7. Using the rim of a jar, create circular layers in the cake. (See page 10)

8. Place 1 layer of the cake into each mason jar. Top with a spoonful of frosting. Repeat until the jars are filled to the brim.

9. Sprinkle with cinnamon sugar (if desired). Enjoy!

Pairing **Riesling**
Geil

COOKIE APPLE PIE

🕐 active prep: 20 min   🕐 inactive prep: 1 hour 45 min   🕐 bake time: 15 to 20 min

APPLE LAYER

1 cup sour cream

1 large egg

1 tablespoon vanilla extract

¾ cup sugar

¼ cup packed brown sugar

¼ teaspoon salt

⅓ cup flour

8 small to medium apples, peeled and sliced into ½-inch wedges

TOPPING

⅓ cup flour

¼ cup sugar

¼ cup brown sugar

1 tablespoon cinnamon

½ cup chopped pecans

4 tablespoons butter

Ice cream or whipped cream for serving (optional)

Apple pie is the first dessert I remember my mom baking when I was a child. Every Thanksgiving, she would make her famous "Sour Cream Apple Pie." I thought the words "sour cream" sounded so unappetizing, that I remained resistant to trying it. Finally, my mom talked me into taking just a small bite. I was shocked at the delicious flavor! How had I allowed myself to miss out on this? I don't want the world to miss out on her amazing recipe, so I officially renamed it Cookie Apple Pie!

· ·

MAKES EIGHT SHORT 8-OZ MASON JARS

1. Preheat your oven to 325°F.
2. In a large bowl, combine the sour cream, egg, vanilla, sugar, brown sugar, salt, and flour. Whisk until ingredients are fully blended. Add the apples, and toss them in the mixture until they are completely coated.
3. Distribute the apple mixture into each mason jar.
4. For the topping, combine all the ingredients together in a medium bowl. Crush them with a fork. When the topping is mixed well but still coarse, sprinkle it on top of the apples.
5. Place the mason jars into pans filled with 1 inch of water. Bake the mason jars for 15 to 20 minutes, or until the topping becomes lightly browned.
6. Allow the jars to cool for 45 minutes, then refrigerate for 1 hour to serve chilled.
7. If desired, add ice cream or whipped cream when serving.

Pairing **Gewürztraminer**
Chateau St. Michelle

CRANBERRY APPLE CHEESECAKE

🕐 active prep: 25 min 　 🕐 inactive prep: 1 hour 20 min 　 🕐 bake time: none

CRUST LAYER

2 tablespoons butter

1 cup crushed graham crackers

FRUIT LAYER

2 medium apples, peeled and thinly sliced

1 cup frozen cranberries

¼ cup packed light brown sugar

1 tablespoon lemon juice

1 teaspoon cinnamon

¼ teaspoon nutmeg

1 tablespoon cornstarch

1 cup water

CHEESECAKE LAYER

1 cup sugar

8 ounces cream cheese, room temperature

1 tablespoon ground cinnamon

1½ cups heavy cream

Caramel topping for drizzle

Outside of cooking with my mother, I was often alone with my imagination when I baked—until I met my friend Christin. Seventh grade is a challenging year for girls, but Christin and I always knew the kitchen would be there to help us decompress at the end of the day. We would laugh, listen to music, and get lost for hours at a time making fun and easy dessert recipes: cookies, cakes, brownies . . . you name it. One day, we decided to venture out and take a risk. We told our moms they weren't allowed to help us in mastering our very first cranberry apple cheesecake! We were so proud of our creation. With no Instagram or Facebook back then, we proudly brought our camera into school to show our friends. To this day, that cranberry apple cheesecake is still one of my favorite baking memories.

· ·

MAKES SIX TALL 8-OZ MASON JARS

1. Melt the butter in a microwave-safe bowl by heating it for 30 seconds.
2. In a medium bowl, drizzle the melted butter over the crushed graham crackers. Stir until the graham crackers are evenly coated.
3. Sprinkle the graham cracker crust into the mason jars. Do not press the graham crackers to the bottom of the jar, so as not to make it too firm.
4. Combine all the ingredients for the fruit layer in a medium skillet (cast iron is ideal). Bring the mixture to a boil for 1 to 2 minutes over medium-high heat, stirring constantly.
5. Reduce the mixture to a simmer. Stir about every 20 to 30 seconds until it thickens. This should take about 4 to 5 minutes.
6. Remove the mixture from the heat and allow it to cool for 20 minutes.
7. Meanwhile, combine all the cheesecake ingredients (except for the caramel topping) in a large bowl. Beat the ingredients on high for 1 to 2 minutes, or until soft peaks begin to form.
8. Distribute the apple-cranberry mixture into each mason jar, followed by the cheesecake layer. Drizzle each jar with caramel syrup.
9. Refrigerate each jar for 1 hour before enjoying.

Pairing **Josh Cellars Rosé**
Joseph Carr

PEPPERMINT COCOA MOUSSE

🕐 active prep: 30 min   🕐 inactive prep: 30 min   🕐 bake time: none

CHOCOLATE MOUSSE LAYER

2 cups semisweet chocolate chips

1¾ cups heavy cream

¼ teaspoon salt

2 teaspoons unflavored, powdered gelatin

2 tablespoons water

PEPPERMINT LAYER

1 box (3.25 ounces) instant vanilla pudding mix

3 cups heavy cream

¼ teaspoon nutmeg

½ cup sugar

½ teaspoon mint extract

Red food coloring (optional)

GANACHE LAYER

1 cup semisweet chocolate chips

3 tablespoons shortening

During my last year of college, I would purchase an extra-large iced peppermint mocha every single day before class. It's a surprise my blood pressure wasn't through the roof! After finally overcoming my severe caffeine addiction, I decided it would be easier on my blood pressure and my wallet to enjoy a chilled peppermint chocolate flavored dessert on occasion, rather than to indulge in a daily beverage. Now, I'll take this delicious dessert over a cup of coffee any day!

. . . .

MAKES EIGHT TALL 8-OZ MASON JARS

1. In a microwave-safe bowl, heat the chocolate chips, heavy cream, and salt in the microwave for 1 minute. Stir thoroughly. Continue heating the chocolate in the microwave for 15-second cycles, stirring thoroughly in between, until the chocolate is melted completely.

2. In a small microwave-safe bowl, stir together the gelatin and the water. The gelatin will turn into a gel-like solid. Heat the gelatin in the microwave for 15 seconds so it melts. The gelatin may have a strong vinegar-like smell, but this will not be present in the flavor of the mousse.

3. Immediately stir and pour the melted gelatin into the melted chocolate before it hardens. Stir the mixture thoroughly.

4. Distribute the chocolate mousse into the jars. The chocolate will still be very runny. Allow the jars to cool for about 30 minutes.

5. For the peppermint layer, beat the vanilla pudding mix, heavy cream, nutmeg, sugar, and peppermint extract on high until stiff peaks begin to form. Stir in the red food coloring and distribute into each jar.

6. Refrigerate the jars while you prepare the ganache layer.

7. In a microwave-safe bowl, heat the chocolate chips and shortening for 30 seconds and stir thoroughly. Continue heating the chocolate chips and shortening for 15 seconds at a time, stirring between each cycle.

8. Allow the ganache to cool for 5 minutes, then drizzle on top of the jars.

9. Keep the jars refrigerated until you are ready to enjoy.

 **Are You Game? Shiraz**
Fowles Wines

74

PUMPKIN PIE CHEESECAKE

🕐 active prep: 15 min   🕐 inactive prep: 1 hour 40 min   🕐 bake time: 35 to 40 min

CRUST

2 tablespoons butter

1 cup crushed graham crackers

CHEESECAKE LAYER

16 ounces cream cheese, room temperature

1 cup sugar

2 large eggs

2 teaspoons vanilla

1 cup canned pumpkin

2 teaspoons pumpkin pie spice

1 teaspoon cinnamon

Dash ground cloves

¼ teaspoon nutmeg

WHIPPED CREAM LAYER

1 cup heavy cream

¼ cup sugar

½ teaspoon vanilla

Cinnamon sugar for garnish (optional)

The Christmas season features the most scrumptious baking flavors: pumpkins, apples, cloves, cinnamon, peppermint, nutmeg, and more! But, if you're like me, it's so challenging to enjoy these flavors only once a year. If you're having guests over and you can't wait an entire year to enjoy your favorite pumpkin dessert, I've found it's possible to pull off this Pumpkin Spice Cheesecake year-round! It's strong enough to enjoy the rich pumpkin spice flavors, but subtle enough when complemented by the vanilla cheesecake layer.

. . . .

MAKES EIGHT TALL 8-OZ MASON JARS

1. Preheat your oven to 300°F.
2. Melt the butter in a microwave-safe bowl by heating it on high for 30 seconds. Drizzle it over the crushed graham crackers and stir until the graham crackers are evenly coated. Set aside.
3. In a large bowl, combine the cream cheese, sugar, and eggs. Beat until the batter is smooth. Split the batter into 2 separate bowls.
4. In the first bowl, beat in the vanilla. In the second bowl, beat in the pumpkin, pumpkin pie spice, cinnamon, ground cloves, and nutmeg.
5. Begin layering the mason jars by distributing the graham cracker layer, followed by the vanilla batter, topped with the pumpkin batter.
6. Fill a brownie pan with 1 inch of water and place the jars inside. Bake the jars for 35 to 40 minutes, or until the top becomes slightly darker.
7. When the cheesecakes are out of the oven, remove them from the bath and allow them to cool for 40 minutes. Place them in the refrigerator and allow them to set for 1 hour.
8. While the cheesecakes are setting, combine all the ingredients for the whipped cream layer in a large bowl and beat until stiff peaks begin to form, about 2 minutes. Keep refrigerated until you are ready to use it.
9. When the cheesecakes have been chilled, spread the whipped cream on top of each mason jar. Garnish with cinnamon sugar (if desired). Enjoy!

Pairing **Riesling**
Nein Lives

CPSIA information can be obtained at www.ICGtesting.com
Printed in the USA
BVIW12n0030121217
502345BV00019B/46